York
Dales

John Potter

MYRIAD

LONDON

Keld This small village nestles snugly in the hills at the head of Swaledale and stands at the crossroads of the coast-to-coast and Pennine Way long-distance footpaths. The beautiful East Gill Force (left), which is fed by the many becks which run into the river Swale, is 10 minutes' stroll north of the villlage.

Arkengarthdale On the eastern side of the Pennines, Arkengarthdale is well known for its attractive patchwork of fields, drystone walls and traditional stone barns. Arkle Town (right) just east of Langthwaite is seen here from Scotty Hill. Nearby is the Tan Hill Inn – the highest pub in the UK.

Langthwaite The largest settlement in Arkengarthdale, Langthwaite's stone cottages huddle together haphazardly alongside Arkle Beck, three miles north-west of Reeth. The welcoming Red Lion pub was used extensively in the filming of the television series *All Creatures Great and Small*.

Kisdon Hill The limestone mass of Kisdon Hill stands at the western head of Swaledale. This viewpoint is from Kisdon Hill looking south towards Muker with the river Swale meandering through the valley to the left.

Gunnerside Famous for its wildflower meadows, the village of Gunnerside sits at the foot of Gunnerside Gill, just three and a half miles east of Thwaite on the road that links Kirkby Stephen with Richmond. In the far distance, at the head of Swaledale, stands the lofty Great Shunner Fell.

Muker The pretty village of Muker sits proudly above Straw Beck just before it joins the river Swale one mile east of Thwaite. The church of St Mary the Virgin is at the heart of the village. Its beautiful stained glass depicts the surrounding scenery and includes an image of 23 horned sheep – a reference to Psalm 23, *The Lord is my Shepherd.*

Reeth Situated 12 miles
west of Richmond on the
B6270, Reeth was once a
centre for both leadmining and
knitting, and now continues to
be the market town and focal
point for the local community.
The village lies at the junction
of Swaledale and Arkengarthdale. From its elevated position
the spacious, triangular village
green provides stunning views
of the surrounding countryside.
The Swaledale Museum on the
green houses exhibits showing
the heritage of the area;
it is open during the summer
months. The Reeth agricultural
show, a highlight of the local
farming year, is held in August.

Richmond The capital of Swaledale, Richmond is dominated by its majestic castle keep, a well-preserved example of 12th century architecture. The town lies south-west of Scotch Corner on the A6108 and is one of the most beautiful in England, with elegant Georgian houses, cobbled streets and pretty cottage gardens. At the centre of the marketplace is the 12th century chapel of the Holy Trinity, now the regimental museum of the Green Howards.

Hawes The busy market town of Hawes is situated between high fells at the head of Wensleydale, on trans-Pennine A684 that links Northallerton in North Yorkshire to Kendal in Cumbria. Known as the "cattle capital" of Upper Wensleydale, it is Yorkshire's highest market town. This beautiful field barn (right) is close to the town.

Hardraw The village of Hardraw lies one mile north of Hawes almost at the foot of Buttertubs Pass – a spectacular link road over the fells from Wensleydale to Thwaite. The view below shows snow-covered fields on the edge of the village. Hardraw Force (below right) can be accessed from the Green Dragon Inn in the centre of the village.

Gayle Situated just half a mile north of the lively market town of Hawes, Gayle is a quiet and pretty village. At the foot of Sledale, Duerley Beck cascades over a series of limestone steps in the centre of the village before rushing below a packhorse bridge. Much of the upper dale can be seen from the bridge where locals stop to exchange the news of the day and visitors pause to admire the stepped waterfalls. An old cotton mill, which dates from 1776, is sited by the beck, and a causeway leads across meadows to Hawes church.

Askrigg Best known as the setting for the television series *All Creatures Great and Small*, Askrigg sits below the slopes of Askrigg Common on a quiet minor road. The home of the fictional vet James Herriot is in the marketplace.

Bainbridge Overlooked from the east by the remains of a Roman settlement, Bainbridge has a wide and sweeping village green with ancient stocks. The river Bain (the shortest river in England) drains into nearby Semerwater, the largest lake in north Yorkshire.

13

Aysgarth The village of Aysgarth is best known for its spectacular waterfalls on the river Ure that cascade over a set of large limestone steps. A series of delightful riverside walks link the Upper, Middle and Lower Aysgarth Falls. The best view of the Upper Falls is from the 16th-century bridge in the centre of the village.

West Burton The pretty, unspoiled village of West Burton is situated one mile south of Aysgarth on the B6160 at the northern end of Bishopdale. To the east of the village, the glorious West Burton Falls, known locally as Cauldron Falls, are best seen from the footbridge at the north end of West Burton. After heavy rainfall, the picturesque falls become a raging torrent as Walden Beck fills with rainwater.

Middleham Just two miles south of Leyburn on the A6108, Middleham is dominated by its castle, which can be seen for miles around. It was built around 1170 by Robert Fitz Randolph during the reign of Henry II. The keep has 12ft (3.5m) thick walls and is one of the largest in England. Middleham is referred to in the Domesday Book as *Medelai* and there has been a settlement here since Roman times. The village is situated between Coverdale and Wensleydale and is famous as a centre for the training of racehorses.

Castle Bolton The small village of Castle Bolton, five miles west of Leyburn, gets its name from the splendid Bolton Castle. There is a wide green in the centre of the village and an attractive 14th-century church, St Oswald's, nestles in the shadow of the castle. This massive fortress has loomed over Wensleydale since 1379 and can be seen for miles around. It is one of the country's best preserved castles; still in private hands, Mary Queen of Scots was imprisoned here during 1568 and 1569.

West Witton Just four miles west of Leyburn on the A684, West Witton sits comfortably in the lee of Penhill Beacon which, at 1,792ft, dominates the skyline in this part of Wensleydale. The parish church of St Bartholomew dates from the Saxon era and was restored in 1875; the remains of a Saxon cross were discovered during the work. The shallow depth of soil in the churchyard meant that the dead from this neighbourhood were taken to nearby Wensley for burial up until1752.

Howgill Fells The Howgills are a small distinctive group of hills bordered by Sedbergh, Kirkby Stephen and Tebay. The southern half of the Howgills lie in the Yorkshire Dales National Park, whilst the northern Howgills are in Cumbria. In the centre of the range lies Cautley Spout, Britain's highest waterfall, where Red Gill Beck tumbles over the edge of Cautley Crags from the shoulder of the Calf – the highest of the Howgill Fells at 2217ft (676m).

Dentdale With its white-painted houses and softly rounded fells, Dentdale has many of the typical character-istics of the Lake District. Four miles south-east of Sedbergh the pretty village of Dent (left) is actually in Cumbria, although it lies within the Yorkshire Dales National Park. The area boasts the highest mainline railway station in Britain (four miles from the village) and is close to the spectacular viaducts of Arten Gill and Dent Head on the Settle-Carlisle railway line.

Ingleton This pretty market town is set amidst unique limestone uplands. Ingleton nestles in the lee of Ingleborough, one of the famous Three Peaks of the Yorkshire Dales, the others being Pen-y-Ghent and Whernside. The Ingleton waterfalls provide visitors with an amazing series of cascades tumbling down through wooded gorges. White Scar Cave, on the lower slopes of Ingle-borough, is the longest show cave in Britain.

Ingleborough The second highest of the Three Peaks, the dramatic flanks of Ingleborough make it easy to identify even from the far distance. This distinctive mountain is pictured here from just below Runscar Hill, shrouded in low cloud on a bitterly cold winter's day. The lower slopes have many caves and potholes and include the cavernous Gaping Gill Pot on the western flank of the mountain.

Kingsdale The two boulders (left) are in the heart of Three Peaks limestone country. Called the Cheese Press Stones, they remind us of the time when cheese was pressed into shape between large stones to dry out.

Settle The busy town of Settle has a dramatic location between the river Ribble and Castlebergh, an impressive 300ft (91m) limestone crag; its pretty market square is surrounded by 18th and 19th-century houses, shops and eateries – including the Naked Man Café (above). The 72-mile Settle to Carlisle railway line starts from nearby Settle Junction; widely considered the most scenic rail route in Britain, the magnificent Ribblehead Viaduct (left) was built between 1870-1875, is 1200ft long and has 24 arches. From the viaduct there are dramatic views of Whernside and Pen-y-Ghent.

Stainforth The broad ston ledges on either side of the r Ribble close to the bridge provide a popular picnic site visitors, and early spring shov ers swell the rapids as they gush over Stainforth Force.

Clapham This little village is a blissful haven for visitors just off the busy A65 six miles north-west of Settle. It is the perfect base for exploring the remote and beautiful Crum-mackdale and is a focal point for walks to Selside, Austwick and Horton in Ribblesdale.

Horton in Ribblesdale The start and finishing point of the famous Three Peaks Walk, Horton is also a popular stopping-off place for ramblers tackling the Pennine Way. The local cafe provides much more than large pots of Yorkshire tea; it is also the place where Three Peaks' participants clock in and out to register their progress on the walk. Each year there is a large entry of competitors in the famous Three Peaks fell race which takes place during the Horton Gala. The fastest runners will cover the 24-mile distance in just under three hours.

Malham Surrounded by some of Britain's most beautiful limestone landscapes, Malham is very popular with visitors. The village lies just five miles west of Settle and two and a half miles south of Malham Tarn on the Pennine Way. Malham Cove is just three-quarters of a mile north of the village and, at 250ft (76m) high and over 300 yards (275m) long, is a magnificent vertical limestone rockface. Its steep walls provide climbers with some of the best routes in the Pennines. Malham's unique landscape is a result of glacial activity some 15,000 years ago.

Arncliffe At the heart of Littondale, one of the loveliest of all the Dales, Arncliffe is the largest of four settlements which include the village of Litton and the small hamlets of Halton Gill and remote Foxup. Just six miles north-west of Grassington, the village sits comfortably by the river Skirfare on a well-drained gravel delta above the flood plain. Arncliffe has a central wide open green, surrounded by mellow stone cottages. Several large porched barns point to the fact that this is a typical Dales' working community. The days of muck-spreading by hand from horse and cart, and taking hay to the fields on horseback, are distant memories now and a far more familiar sound is that of the quad bike. Littondale was the setting for part of Charles Kingsley's famous children's novel *The Water Babies*.

Halton Gill At the northern end of Littondale, the hamlet of Halton Gill sits beside the infant river Skirfare, which is fed by Cosh Beck, Foxup Beck and Hesleden Beck.

Littondale Of the four settlements in the lush valley of Littondale, Foxup (below) is the most remote. It is situated near Foxup Beck on the river Skirfare, just a stone's throw from Halton Gill.

Gordale Scar Just one mile north-east of Malham, the limestone escarpment opens up into a huge rocky gorge known as Gordale Scar. This massive ravine was gouged out of the landscape by melting glaciers during the Ice Age; the 100m high overhanging cliffs make it one of the most spectacular sights in the Dales. Gordale Beck cascades over two waterfalls as it makes its way through the gorge. The beck then leaves the gorge and tumbles over a limestone outcrop into a deep pool.

Littondale and Wharfedale from Hill Castle Scar This photograph was taken just a few metres from the Dales Way long-distance footpath, between Kettlewell and Grassington, just north-east of the delightful village of Conistone in Wharfedale. The view towards Hawkswick Moor and Middlesmoor Pasture is quite breathtaking, especially when weather systems are racing across the dales, creating atmospheric and dramatic skies.

Yockenthwaite Yockenthwaite is a tiny settlement in Langstrothdale, the upper valley of the Wharfe, about two and a half miles north-west of Buckden. In Norman times Langstrothdale Chase was a hunting preserve for game and deer, with its own forest laws, courts, punishments and privileges. Now the upper dale is a haven of solitude.

Hubberholme This tiny village is located on the Dales Way four and a half miles from Kettlewell and is famous for the beautiful St Michael's church and the George Inn, pictured here beyond the bridge. Hubberholme was the favourite village of the writer JB Priestley. Literary pilgrims visit the village to visit The George where the novelist could often be found enjoying the local ale. The church-yard is the last resting place for his ashes. The choir stalls and the pews in St Michael's were made in 1934 by Robert Thompson, the "Mouseman" of Kilburn. His distinctive trademark – a carved mouse – appears on all his work.

31

Great Whernside This rugged hill dominates the skyline to the east of Buckden. Not to be confused with Whernside (one of the Three Peaks further to the west) this massive hill stands at the junction of Wharfedale and Coverdale. It reaches a height of 2310ft and marks an abrupt change in the landscape from the lush pastures in the valley below.

Buckden The village of Buckden, four miles north of Kettlewell on the B6160, is very popular with walkers; paths lead from the village in all directions, making it the perfect base for exploring Wharfedale with its glorious scenery. The annual Buckden Pike Fell Race is a great draw for runners.

Cray The little hamlet of Cray nestles at the southern end of Bishopdale one and a half miles north of Buckden. It is the starting point for many walks and its famous inn, The White Lion, is the highest pub in Wharfedale. Cray Gill runs into the river Wharfe a couple of miles south of the village and is fed by several smaller gills which cascade over rocky outcrops forming beautiful waterfalls. All are within easy walking distance of the village along well-marked footpaths.

Kettlewell In the shadow of Great Whernside 13 miles north of Skipton, Kettlewell is popular with potholers, climbers and walkers. Its buildings are clustered close to Cam Beck, near where it joins the river Wharfe. The Scarecrow Festival in the village has become a popular community event. The fields above lie just south of the village and were photographed from a footpath just above Crookacre Wood. The long-distance footpath, the Dales Way, which links Ilkley to Windermere, runs along the valley bottom at this point.

Kilnsey The tiny village of Kilnsey lies three miles north of Grassington on the B6160 in the heart of Wharfedale. It nestles in the shadow of Kilnsey Crag (right), a dramatic peak much loved by climbers. The Kilnsey agricultural show is held every year on the Tuesday after the August Bank Holiday. The long-distance footpath the Dales Way passes close by and pony-trekking is available from the village of Conistone. There is also fly-fishing and a nature trail at Kilnsey Park Trout Farm. The very popular Tennants Arms provides a warm welcome.

Linton Seven miles north of Skipton this characterful village consists of stone cottages built in clusters around the village green, which is seen here with the Fontaine Inn in the background. Fontaine Hospital, also on the green, was built in 1721 as almshouses for six poor men or women and stands close to a pretty stepping-stone bridge across the beck. Riverside paths carry walkers along both banks.

Grassington The largest settlement in upper Wharfedale, the village of Grassington owes its development to its close proximity to the point where two historically important roads cross in the dale

– the B6160 from Ilkley to Buckden and the B6265 Skipton to Pateley Bridge. Grassington has many charming features including a cobbled square complete with an ornate water pump. The village grew rapidly with the opening of the Yorkshire Dales Railway to Threshfield in 1901 which brought in settlers who worked in nearby Skipton or in the rapidly developing local limestone quarries.

Burnsall Ten miles north-west of Ilkley, Burnsall is famous for its five-arched bridge which spans the Wharfe. Built by Sir William Craven, who also restored the parish church and endowed the local grammar school, the bridge is probably the most photographed in the Dales. Every August Burnsall hosts the Feast Sports (named after the Feast of St Wilfrid), England's oldest fell race. This event is hugely popular with locals and visitors alike and there is a wonderful carnival atmosphere with the bridge thronged with spectators.

Hebden The small village of Hebden lies on the road to Pateley Bridge and Nidderdale about two miles east of Grassington. Located in an upland valley it is surrounded by rocky crags and picturesque waterfalls. Hebden sits proudly above its beck within a narrow gorge, which is unusual for this area in exposing dark gritstone rock rather than the more familiar limestone. Hebden Beck runs through the village as it makes its way down to the river Wharfe.

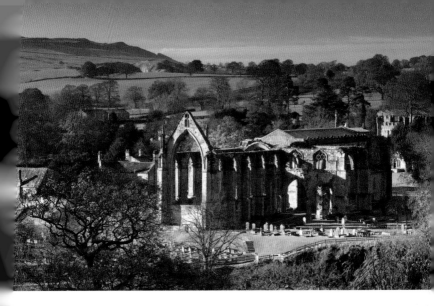

Bolton Abbey Bolton Bridge, on the A59 just five miles west of Skipton, is the gateway to Wharfedale. It is just a stone's throw from Bolton Abbey, a beautiful Augustinian priory. The abbey was founded in 1151 on land given by Lady Alice de Romille of Skipton Castle. In the early 14th century the abbey was

reduced to ruins by Scottish raiders although the nave of the church was still used as a parish church until the Dissolution of the Monasteries, from 1536 onwards. Bolton Abbey is very popular with visitors, many of whom linger close to the monastic buildings, often choosing to picnic and spend a day by the river. Further upstream, along a nature trail, can be found Barden Bridge and the beautifully sited Barden Tower, which was built in 1485 by Lord Henry Clifford, and restored by Lady Anne Clifford in 1658-59. Another popular spot is "the Strid" – a narrow chasm through which the river Wharfe gushes – and the enchanting Valley of Desolation, with its waterfalls and wooded glades.

Pateley Bridge The town's narrow main street is dominated by elegant dark gritstone buildings. On either side there are pretty cobbled alleyways and passages which lead to hidden and quaint courtyards.

Ripley Castle This fortified manor house sits on the eastern edge of the village of Ripley three miles north of Harrogate. The 1,700 acre estate, which includes the village, is owned by the Ingilby family who have lived in the castle for 700 years.

Skipton Regarded as the southern gateway to the Dales, Skipton is located in Airedale, south of Malham and 22 miles north-west of Leeds. The Leeds-Liverpool Canal lies just a few minutes walk from Skipton's busy high street. In the 1750s Skipton was a thriving centre for the wool trade. By the end of the century the development of the canal helped establish the worsted cloth industry in the town. Skipton Castle is one of the best-preserved medieval castles in England.

Fountains Abbey One of the most popular attractions in Yorkshire, Fountains Abbey and Studley Royal is a huge estate which includes the largest ruined abbey in England, together with a spectacular Georgian water garden and deer park.

West Tanfield The village of West Tanfield sits proudly beside the river Ure on the western edge of the Yorkshire Dales, six miles north of Ripon on the A6108. Crossing the impressive stone bridge over the river, one cannot fail to be moved by the glorious aspect the village has beside the dark waters of the river Ure and the surrounding countryside. The skyline of the village is dominated by both the Marmion Tower and the Church of St Nicholas.

Jervaulx Abbey The beautiful ruins of Jervaulx Abbey lie between Masham and Leyburn. The abbey was founded in 1156 by Cistercian monks who moved from Fors, higher up the valley, in search of better weather. The abbey was ruined after the Dissolution of the Monasteries in 1537 and much of its stonework used in other local buildings.

Masham This peaceful market town is situated midway between Ripon and Leyburn on the A6108. Pronounced "Massum", the town has many attractions; its generous cobbled marketplace is surrounded by elegant Georgian houses and stone cottages.

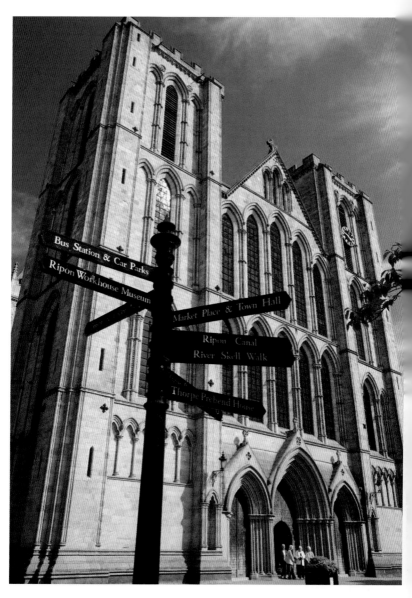

pon The small city of Ripon lies the north of Knaresborough on banks of the river Ure and is rerded as a gateway to the eastern les. Behind its attractive riverside uses is Ripon Cathedral. St Wilfred st built a church here over 1300 ars ago but the present building the fourth to be established on is site. The church did not achieve thedral status until 1836 when the ocese of Ripon was created. The estern front and towers of the thedral are fine examples of early nglish church architecture. The ecorated nave was built in the 15th entury. Ripon has three museums – e Courthouse Museum, the Prison nd Police Museum and the Workouse Museum of Poor Law. The Courthouse Museum featured in Yorkshire Television's popular series *Heartbeat*. The canal at Ripon was constructed to connect Ripon to the river Ure at Oxclose Lock and then via the river Ouse to the Humber and the other waterways of Yorkshire. The cut runs for approximately two and a half miles (4km).

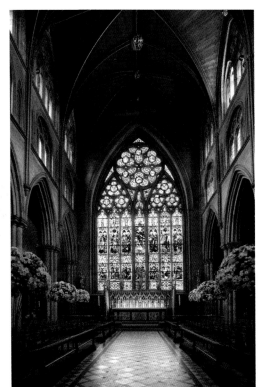

Appletreewick and Simon's Seat Fantastic panoramic views can be enjoyed from Rowan Tree Crag on the lower slopes of Barden Fell just south of Burnsall.